The Book of Accident

Akron Series in Poetry

Akron Series in Poetry
Elton Glaser, Editor

Barry Seiler, *The Waters of Forgetting*

Raeburn Miller, *The Comma After Love: Selected Poems of Raeburn Miller*

William Greenway, *How the Dead Bury the Dead*

Jon Davis, *Scrimmage of Appetite*

Anita Feng, *Internal Strategies*

Susan Yuzna, *Her Slender Dress*

Raeburn Miller, *The Collected Poems of Raeburn Miller*

Clare Rossini, *Winter Morning with Crow*

Barry Seiler, *Black Leaf*

William Greenway, *Simmer Dim*

Jeanne E. Clark, *Ohio Blue Tips*

Beckian Fritz Goldberg, *Never Be the Horse*

Marlys West, *Notes for a Late-Blooming Martyr*

Dennis Hinrichsen, *Detail from* The Garden of Earthly Delights

Susan Yuzna, *Pale Bird, Spouting Fire*

John Minczeski, *Circle Routes*

Barry Seiler, *Frozen Falls*

Elton Glaser and William Greenway, eds., *I Have My Own Song for It: Modern Poems of Ohio*

Melody Lacina, *Private Hunger*

George Bilgere, *The Good Kiss*

William Greenway, *Ascending Order*

Roger Mitchell, *Delicate Bait*

Lynn Powell, *The Zones of Paradise*

Dennis Hinrichsen, *Cage of Water*

Sharmila Voorakkara, *Fire Wheel*

Vern Rutsala, *How We Spent Our Time*

Clare Rossini, *Lingo*

Beckian Fritz Goldberg, *The Book of Accident*

The Book of Accident

Beckian Fritz Goldberg

The University of Akron Press
Akron, Ohio

All inquiries and permission requests should be addressed to the Publisher,
The University of Akron Press, 374B Bierce Library, Akron, Ohio 44325-1703.

Acknowledgments

American Alphabets: Twenty-Five Contemporary Poets: "Nights in the Constellation of
the Twin-Hearted Prisoner," "Third Body," "Twentieth-Century Children (2),"
"Twentieth-Century Children (5): Blood-Kissing." *The Clackamas Review*: "Dark-
room," "The Last Courtship in the Book," "Last Erotica." *Crab Orchard Review*:
"Memory on the Shoulders of the Gaze." *Field*: "Body of the Hour," "Summer
Heats like the Needle in Its Chosen Skin," "Twentieth-Century Children," "Twenti-
eth-Century Children (5): Blood-Kissing." *Hayden's Ferry Review*: "How He Became
Conservator of the Meadow," "Lightning-Wolf." *The Indiana Review*: "Life Story,"
"The Life and Times of Skin-Girl," "The New Boy-Wonders," "Torture Boy's
Watch, Burn Boy's Boat of Souls," "Twentieth-Century Children (2)." *The Iowa
Review*: "Washed in the River." *The Journal*: "Nights with the Star-Ladle over the
House." *Lake Effect*: "Annunciation." *The Massachusetts Review*: "Dialogue: Memory
and Forgetting," "Nights in the Constellation of the Twin-Hearted Prisoner," "Sud-
den Masters." *Manthology*: "Torture Boy at the Easter Confest, Repentance Creek."
The Onset Review: "Forest-Body (2)," "Hummingbird," "Lost Tribe." *Quarterly West*:
"Relic," "Skin Girl's Tattoo." *Washington Square*: "Nights in the Constellation of the
Tree Stepping from Its Robe," "The Set Glistening."
Some of the poems in this volume previously appeared in a chapbook, *Twentieth-
Century Children* (Bloomington, Ind.: Graphic Design Press, 1999).

LIBRARY OF CONGRESS CATALOGING-IN-PUBLICATION DATA

Goldberg, Beckian Fritz.
  The Book of Accident / Beckian Fritz Goldberg.— 1st ed.
    p. cm. — (Akron series in poetry)
  ISBN-13: 978-1-931968-35-5 (alk. paper)
  ISBN-10: 1-931968-35-7 (alk. paper)
  1. Title.
  PS3557.O3556B66 2006
  811'.54—DC22

                    2006002333

Cover image: Center detail from Steven Assael, *At Mother*, 2001, oil, wood panel,
canvas, and steel, 110 x 156 x 42 inches. © Steven Assael, courtesy of Forum Gallery,
New York.

Contents

one

Twentieth-Century Children   3
Darkroom   4
Twentieth-Century Children (2)   5
The New Boy-Wonders   6
At the Dream Birth   7
Dialogue: Memory and Forgetting   8
Nights in the Constellation of the Twin-Hearted Prisoner   9
Forest-Body   11
Easy   12
Nights in the Preparation of a Journey   13
A Thousand Words   15
Torture Boy at the Easter Confest, Repentance Creek   16
How He Became Conservator of the Meadow   18
The White Hill   19
Lightning-Wolf   21
Amnesia (1)   22
Amnesia (2)   23

two

Third Body   27
Skin Girl among the Roses   28
Last Erotica   30
Torture Boy's Watch, Burn Boy's Boat of Souls   33
Wolf in the Cradle   34
Twentieth-Century Children (3):
        Meditation on the Mother of Black Trees   35
The Absolute   37
The Black Drop   38
Prologue, Epilogue   39
Body of the Hour   40
Again, Spring Speaks in a Dream   41
Twentieth-Century Children (4)   42
The Fourth Body   43
The Boys at the Grave of Poe   44
Memoir of the Middle of the Book   46

three

Annunciation   51
The Life and Times of Skin Girl   53
Souls   58
Lost Tribe   59
Burn Boy's Celestial   60
Torture Boy's Cradle   62
The Set Glistening   64
Warning   67
Nights with the Star-Ladle over the House   68

four

Memory on the Shoulders of the Gaze   71
Warning (2)   72
The Torture and Burn Boys Entered the Video Arcade   73
Twentieth-Century Children (5): Blood-Kissing   75
Forest-Body (2)   76
Nights in the Constellation of the Tree Stepping from Its Robe   77
Hummingbird   79
Life Story   80
Summer Heats like the Needle in Its Chosen Skin   81
Sudden Masters   83
Relic   86
The Courtship at the End of the Book   87
Skin Girl's Tattoo   89
Washed in the River   90

My friend, we suffer from the disease
we have not yet contracted.
—Baudelaire

For Dick

one

Twentieth-Century Children

We were born in the light
of the war of the Gargantuas.
We were born into the picture
as others might be born into the world,
with the bloom of a giant ape foot
over Tokyo, with the blink of
the Lizard Men in New York. Not God,
but the God-hairs brushing close—and the fire
up first like a fat mutant
gold cicada
which had slept in the earth
on the secret installations.
We were bathed
in the glow of the beast
from 20,000 fathoms, the arctic
flash of calving ice,
our bright fur groomed
under a mother's tongue that clicked
like starlodes. We
were created in the image
of the image of the glazed
stare of God, its half-lives,
its dream-kitchens of gold-
flecked tile, its backyard
bottle trees and common wrens, its
television, television
glitter on our faces, other
on our faces, other
falling on our beds, utter
dying we were the picture of,
an eye for an eye,
an eye for a mouth.

Darkroom

Everything is in the process of recurring:
Colts in the darkroom,
those clarifying blots with jaws,
disjointed spines—

The sow from Malinovka
born without eye sockets—

These aren't our children.
Last night, she would tell him,
I gave birth to a son in my sleep.

He was an ordinary wolf boy.

But why reason with the God of Pictures?

And why say to a man, "The accident
was so long ago, why can't you forget?"

Twentieth-Century Children (2)

Everything she finds she drags home:
the cat, the ruined boots, the rusted knife,
the legless doll—

Can I keep it? And the boy is packing
a snowball in the freezer to save
for August. The sisters, no wiser, are
keeping warm

some small blue eggs on a cotton ball
constellation under mother's make-up lamp.
Things will stay.

Things will wait. This child's
America cooks up forever, and the stars
get pasted in their Book of Looks—

This light.
This word.
This favored found stone they sleep with.
And the moth they've sealed in

a plastic pin box and buried beneath
their folded summer shirts, so that someday
when they leave or when

they marry, they will find it
still, thing
and no more
the dream around it—

The New Boy-Wonders

They would have found the place earlier
except the one with *Torture* spelled out on his T-shirt
was afraid of lightning,
the arm shagging after him,
its zag into white time,

Orchid Town:
kids out on the streets blossoming
their cigarette cherries,
dogs staring from the windows like mothers

wondering, What's that year slinking by the porch?

When they reintroduced us to the wild,
one said, we lost track
we forgot our movie stars
we forgot our fire-scars
we forgot poetry.

In the next flash a house stepped
onto the far hill
and the meadow was licked

clean as the face of an object—
the metal crate
the experiment slept in, hush-hush—

the wolf boy left by accident
in the middle of someone's field.

At the Dream Birth

There is a second body:
The palms fill with mud
in the middle of the night,
the mirror takes a bath, the black's poultice
draws poison from the pores. Honey from the pores,
thick as meditation.

In the first,
in its heart,
you remember the birth of the wolf boy
and how, even after you woke to
the light of myth, the upright
spaces, that happiness lingered,
it lingered, black drop,

it will have nothing to do with time.

Dialogue: Memory and Forgetting

Naked and pale, pale as the plucked end of light,
is this your only body, this

you cover with mud, with fur, with sweet oil,
a sheet?

You drive it to work and back. And on the way
it comes to you, wolves

come from the book of snow
of childhood, fur taking in the weak
light, the light so low

it's important
not to know what next,

what goes out—
Here, I said,
it's a world where no one has to love you.

But they do.

Nights in the Constellation of the Twin-Hearted Prisoner

for R.B.G.

Then the body said   Did you love me   Prove you loved me.

And I said to the notebook   Nothing but you, the horizon—

And it was true.

I was thinking of the face
    my mother used to carve on the apple
    before she gave it to me to eat—

I was, as always, faithful to my memory, my very
    last . . .

And then there are dreams that become memories,
    my dream of the two prisoners with the same name—
    one in his cell, one missing

and I take the one out and put him beside
    the cell of the missing one

so they'll think he's there—and so far
    this isn't much different from memory, down

to the last detail of the man who wanders
    the prison village at night
    carrying a lamb no one will cook.

Then the body said   Take me with you.

And the childhood knife said   I will take you
    with me, I will smile

you tenderly with me, I will tend you,

the sweet evening said, I
    who wove you and weft you, I will

pour you from one breast to another,
    I will feed your missing, and the blue
    solaces said, And

where my alone meets your alone, I will,
    oh Lamb in Arms,

yes, I loved you, Husband Skin,
    husband

like guilt when I came I was yours forever.

Forest-Body

The infant matches his front feet, back feet,
says, *You see how easy birth is.*
What were you afraid of?

Fear: You'd better not tell him you love him.

This is the mother-story, the sweetheart-story,
the friend's story. . . .

He is my old, my forest body,
that alone—

Years before it can walk.
Speak. *Love throws its leg across.*

Easy

Most of all Torture Boy loved the lepers
in the Bible movies, long after the story
faded he remembered the mother and daughter,
stump-armed, veiled because there was no
nose left on the face or maybe the lips were

skinless. Maybe their nipples . . .
He thought the disease was genius. Eating
away the form until the soul fled into the last
safe skin it would ever know.

In his town there were only a couple men
with missing fingers and one with a fake
leg. One swan, too, who got
caught in the fence. A mute swan they called
Bix though no one knew why. *Why*

grass is greene, or why our blood is red
Are mysteries none have reach'd into. . . .
All he knew was swans smelled even
worse than chickens. Every once in a while
at night a wolf or fox would come and leave
only feathers. That was the easy way, your blood
and bones inside another body, but

the leper's—inside nothing.

Nights in the Preparation of a Journey

For the new moon, I put on fear,
its blue whiskers bright as night rain
bouncing off the muzzle—

the sting of camphor in the lining,
old mask
from an old festival
no longer celebrated: A daughter's

ritual in the attic, someone's
ballet shoes, wood in the toes, clack
them together . . .

Then the photograph of a boy in the woods
wearing my cheekbones, but not my eyes,
and the four darknesses—
eyes, time, place, and luck—

to stop us where it does. Right
at the beginning of the Book of Accident,
at the Prayer for Confusion
and the Bewilderment of Want.

Here's where you can't go on.

So you go back.
And your father runs in his sleep again.
And your mother spends another year
being queen of the left-handed compliment,
as in:

"Not only is he a wolf boy, but he's also radioactive."

"Not only is the moon a dish, but it's also a cheese."

A Thousand Words

Soon everyone claimed to have seen it,
the four-legged boy in a bristle of light,
that wolf nose—

For proof, the picture
taken by the Conservator of the Meadow
of a running body, the silver

trace-tails in its three wakes.
The blur coming from the trees
was not

in white time or blue time
but in the curve
forgetfulness shades,

a world
stilled in this one, held

in this one—always about
to turn toward us:

the ice, the windows, the green car—
and the father beside it, what year. . . .

Torture Boy at the Easter Confest, Repentance Creek

The year Jimmy had four pearls
inserted in the shaft of his cock,
Torture Boy took tusks carved from pau-pau shell
and pierced them through his upper lip,
wore them for five days before
his gums were too eroded, and signed
the Mutation Manifesto anyway. Outer
Change Is Inner, would say the goddam
T-shirt. He'd laugh and then begin
to worry that when he laughed he was
ugly.

There was a bluebird one morning,
something he'd never seen, and
it made him gasp. What a girl
I am, he thought, and put beetles
in all the sleeping bags and, in
Jimmy's, itching powder. That
made him laugh

and that made him ugly.
And that made him want to hang himself
and come.
            Instead, he took his knife
down to the creek where he'd think
of the old lady living in a cabin
down the road. She'd always smile
and give a little wave in that old
lady way that pissed him off.

When it got dark, yeah, he'd buzz
past her place on his dirt bike,
then back nice and close and then
around the fucking house. He'd scare her
before he'd use the knife to cut
a lock of hair first
then all her stupid old lady buttons.
Yeah. She'd
cry. He'd want to be merciful,

so he'd explain how the way back
was light already, the water so cold
it stung his face awake. She'd understand
he was just an instrument. He was good.
Felt fresh, fresh as the day he was born.
Yeah. And they'd laugh. . . .

How He Became Conservator of the Meadow

The meadow used to take care of itself,
the parting and lying down,
the bending and silvering,
the propagation of yarrows—

the visitation of wings,
the mimicry of sashes in the dusky hour,
and the clammy perfumes that came

from the opening and shutting of spaces.
He could feel, as night was
coming through, the meadow
holding his feet. This was before
the song sparrow became extinct,

and the blue pike,
and the ruby terror-flower,
the pride of June. And before

there was shopping nearby and
a fireworks factory—so suddenly it seemed
that a man born in the twentieth century
could not finish his pastoral elegy. . . .

The White Hill

The eye would fall on him at night in bed,
the camera, its whir, pointing
its tiny light, as if his sleep would
open up like a woman and let it
in. But in

was only water, sometimes, or being lost
and then in woods where soldiers were hiding
or, once, a monster. The clearing was his own
soft cheek,

lit up like a moon on the pillow,
that flickered in the den in the morning,
curtains closed, portable screen
set up in front of the bookshelves. Father's
smoke would roll down like a white ray
where the door was cracked open.

Sometimes the eyelids twitched, the hand
dropped over the side of the bed or the
mouth hung open. He didn't know that body,
the boy thought, though it was his own:
the nose, the dark hair, dark down . . .

At dinner father would lecture
over a bourbon on the perils of reproduction.
Mother would look far away.

There was a shot of him looking up
squinting and blinking then a look away
from the camera—he rolled over and buried
his face in the pillow, pulled up the sheets.
He was a white hill. He was a star, a star

even the nights he had fevers and melted
into himself, met a wild dog in a meadow
and prayed it would not, even for a half-second,
cross his face.

Lightning-Wolf

for Hershman John

Then the wolf boy was living
in a metal crate in a snowbound pen
in someone's field.

Spring came.
It came through a hole in the top of the crate.
Heady as the vanilla bogs,

east, which belonged to
the Conservator of the Meadow.
And the ice melted

all at once with the hiss of a bootstruck match,
with a large and sloppy kiss—
The crate floated like an ark
and there were showers,
thunder,

and the 4,000-volt bolt belting
the glitter-to-shit out of the bright box
and he was born again

crackling by his short hairs,
a life so quick it was
memory before it passed,
pissed itself

before the body. As before the executioner
throws the switch.

As before the animal
finds the door.

Amnesia (1)

Nightwater in the small fountain,
air wavering before the magnet,

and I don't know why I listen to you,
Scare-Girl:

Your eyes are bigger
than your head. What to do
when you open them—

but black out. Then
friends call at two or three
in the morning,   Did you get home all right?
And I wonder—

if they hear me—if
they can hear me—
why do they ask?

Why does a beautiful night like this
fall down me, fall down me,
who loves this world more

than anyone but the demon. . . .

Amnesia (2)

Past, what's wrong with you?

I would have disappeared earlier,
thrown a handful of wicked-self-dust,

but somehow that sadness
from years ago wanted to have
an anniversary—

a candle. Reflection
walked all over the fountain's pond,
upside-down-lantern-green

with wingmeal in it.
It's the nature of now

the gleam where you look is not where it came from.
All that now

is good for
is beginning another story
like the old ones

that began, Let's take the children out to the woods
and leave them.

two

Third Body

Because the past is in love the way
the future is not,
the child I abandoned
I abandoned

without language: a blood ache
this silence
like my mother's childhood,

this her, red-budded dress in my dream,
this me, this it,

this not-a-hair, not-a-whisper,
this squat—

child on its haunches, enchanted
the way the lost have to be

to be, after such a longing.

Skin Girl among the Roses

Mother's back slicks against the knot
of the blue halter   she's deadheading
the roses   kill me   before my love comes
to this   the little black dwarf she is   floating
over the bushes in the afternoon

If I slipped out the back door into
a smoke and then on to the Ink Palace
or stole the car and drove all night
and got to the sun by breakfast, big
sun sliding off its plate

gold   Mother's in love with the Red
Can Can   a miniature so rare she says there is
no photo of it   my God just
blow my fucking head off if I come
to this   here comes the grill: where are you going
who are you going with what time
will you be home never taking her eyes away
from the pink Abbandonata

I'd love if she didn't: I don't know   around
   friends   whenever

what are their names do I know them

Larry Moe and Curly

That's it get in the house smart mouth
you're not going anywhere

Red Can Can   Abba Dabba   A Coeur Vert

O cover me with a balm or roses red seas
and thorns that orange and grenadine that
California sunrise the blooming dead jellyfish
and shoot me full of odor
and pinch off my dead and press me into attar
and bring into me bees   red bees
and keep me busy

Last Erotica

Love does not exist in and of itself as a substance:
it is the accident of substance.
—Dante

Stay with me, your body in
my body—

heat said. Heat said,
Your eyelid, my tongue.

But the snake left

his skin hollow as if
he'd been seen through.

I'd leave skin, too,
and wear night altogether,
sweet, vampiric, limbless, and complete. . . .

Don't, night said,

talk to me about the body
until you can wrap your legs
around your ears and bug-walk
your flesh to its diminishment—

Listen. Those cicadas
were once boys

who wouldn't stop singing love songs
long enough to eat
or drink,

so women buried them.

***

Brother hum, all night the fits
and starts
can't

cross this silence which is a burning one.

So,
quantum foam.

So, people writing letters.

So—saints
come and go on the beast of voice.

—I'm not your soul, says my leg.

Don't talk to me about the body.
Cups of the eyes. Hinges of the eyelids . . .

oil of parting places. Last night,
halfway through, the body disappeared,
what I'd been kissing . . .

I had looked up

***

and when
I looked back down there was nothing
under me—

flatness no roundness no
moistness, and I—left

at the point of utter rain:
That the mind that is the body could do this.
That the skin

is like any other record, stone, paper,
microchip, alley wall. . . .

We can't bear you anymore, the women said.

Your eye like the mouth of my deepest, your
monsoon swirls, fold of my fold my

beat my throttle—who could stop singing?

Torture Boy's Watch, Burn Boy's Boat of Souls

What kind of boy was this
watching over the Orchid Town swannery—

He was the kind, he'd marry a girl and then say,
"I hate your mother,
your sister, too, and all the shitbirds
you came from." Oh, then
you'd know the ache of love. . . .

But first he'd meet the boy at the wolf-rock
lighting gasoline rags
and they'd wonder together if the story
they were in were true,

the story where the burning rag floated
across the water, and the fat tantaras
of the swans set off

a knifing lamentation in the woods
as the rag boat lit the other shore
and died—

the shape of the wolf flared out,
the shape of the boy flared out
dark,

weird as an accident in the Bible—
the chapter where God, having lost
his lover in the trees, stumbles

in verse 18
across forgetfulness . . .

Wolf in the Cradle

Tonight the intoxicants are stopped at the door,
and the first man's nightmare
is the second man's walking around.
Lilacs in the tumbler.
Dream, you don't know your place.
Dream, you don't know—

You can rock a wolf in his cradle,
but you can't make him think.

Mist in the keyhole.
An eye for an eye.

Body, you don't know who you are,
little swarm
where the skin was.

Twentieth-Century Children (3):
Meditation on the Mother of Black Trees

The day the mother stands in a pool of gasoline
and lights her oldest boy, his small brother,
the girl, then

goes up herself in
one blue tonguing

and the firemen arrive
and weep, it's still spring, and inexplicable

things happen all the time
now—this orange blossom

held up too close to
the minute, it could
explode—melt—marry—float away

to a day those boys put a firecracker
in the mouth of a kitten

and the sad willing thing lived . . .

Nothing explains the body
at the mercy
of something it houses and can't
see into, black

mother of black trees growing
in the crux of the fire lake—or the gold
crown left in the belly of the empty

fragrant boat. Like that,
a night detail
crosses over to the day. What was it—

the child I had, the nap of fur,
flower of skin. . . .

Flower, no love
but the love that's borne you this far
can bear you now.

The Absolute

Finally I gave up and became the rose,
all those treacherous peaks of my sleep
around me and only one eye
in the fold . . . Such a time,

flouncing its dress, rests, essence—
Inhumanly sweet. Green serpent head,
tongue flame, blood-lettuce, easing
bodice, breasts on the balcony,

breasts on the balcony. No one
to say where I came from
wasn't good enough—

My lips of many mansions,
gorget upon gorget, and slit
upon slit where the blade pulls out
and the plush rushes up—

No one to repeat
what I said when I was drunk.
No one

to object to the recounting and recounting
of the fragrances of the tower of you—

Absolutely
no one to be a woman

in the life that had already
the look of pure attachment,

fire to the stalk.

The Black Drop

I can only imagine when they take out your heart
and put it in the pan set out
for the death-wolf, also known
as threshing wolf,

that I'll evaporate, I'll have
come to nothing
like a car on a bridge over a lake
and a child waving down to the shadow car
in the shadow girders crossing the water at exactly
the same speed, and when both

the blob and she hit shore,
everyone's gone, outlived their children,
and it's now again and now again and now again,

the setting out. Of grief
from duration.

Prologue, Epilogue

Because when he sensed me he kept
his eye on the ground—
In buildings took the stairs to
avoid me, tranced by the violet
gleam of his flews, so

the more he withdrew the more
space I became, and hair,
and beauty, and therein
conceived the wolf boy
whose memory is so short
each time he sees my face he cries

at the miraculous reunion—

Body of the Hour

To say, *the soul*

is like saying, *the clock
lost its body and went on ticking.*

Shadow-body, this one
who lived behind the bat-faced
bone of the pelvis

raised in the slicked-back hackle of blood. . . .

To say, comfort me now in the hour
of my loss is

to be the hour, always.
To be Lord Almost.
Mother So-Close.

To be this time each time
you stop—put down the fork
or turn the page and look up:

The meadow in a lather of white
four-o-clocks, the birthmarked
butterfly moving

as if written—erased—written . . .

I remember once in this world
I was an absence,
like you. Like you.

Again, Spring Speaks in a Dream

I know it is a prison
though its dovecotes
sparkle, the walls glow with mosses,

and this silver jetliner
creeps the winding road like a wagon.

I know this country
mantled with fern and green fever
is Vietnam. Quiet,

empty, not a soul in sight, not a flicker
in any window of the gaunt houses
crowded on the mountainside—

When we reach the top, the jet driver says,
we won't be able to speak,
we won't be able to hear.

Green, how long have you been
growing in my room, mystery-fields
of my childhood and its soldiers?

Brother,
how long has it been . . . the back there . . .

—You know time. Time
doesn't have to do a thing
but sit.

Twentieth-Century Children (4)

One night sitting around the meteor pit
outside town, she swore
she could smell the afterlife, this
earth gashed by stars—

out there,
what was left but the insect whine
of boys' dirt bikes seaming the field . . .

She could imagine their far-off swoons of dust
and the zinc taste of their mouths
and what their souls would look like

if there were souls—
like gray tufts of fur snagged on barbed wire—

and then remembered
on such and such a night, so much later,
as if she'd been missing since childhood
and suddenly—

here,
the gorge of solitude . . .

The Fourth Body

And suddenly—
here,
the gorge of solitude . . .

as if she'd been missing since childhood
and then someone said,
You've blossomed.

And the night's spring rush:
I have so much to tell you!

(Was my father a wolf or a man)
(Was my mother a mother or a dream)

So now if I tell you I stand here,
my hands
through the sleeves of the body,

the fourth body—
I can tell you you have no
idea what is the personal

white wolf until
you've seen autumn standing there

—in your place—

holding his purplish scrotum like a sack of leaves.

The Boys at the Grave of Poe

Old snow tucked in the graveyard
to a stone, a stranger's marker, where they crouched,
turned off the flashlights, passed the pipe, its little
rock of hash an orange solitaire. The truck
with the single taillight

had stopped at last
and picked them up. On the road four days
then the squat near the harbor
where the homeless had their blankets and carts,
and the runaway girls were just skanks.

Far away cars were soft
as dresses crushing in the dark. A siren
braying. The pipe was cashed.
A rustle in tree or bush—Torture Boy
waved the beam of the flashlight, and a tondo
of mulberry opened. Black-gray veins.
Suddenly nothing seemed better than the cemetery,
the heavy fruit of dark, the balm within the chill,
and the simple purpose . . .

It was a vigil. They'd catch the Poe Toaster
with his cognac and roses.

But this was not true in the morning,
the groundskeeper with his rake, knuckles
against the nape of his neck. Roses already
black at the lip by the marble monument, its tribute
jar of honey, a lipstick, a penny.

And Burn Boy chanting to the morning
watchman warily, don't touch me
don't touch me don't touch me
over and over like the waves in "Annabel Lee."

Memoir of the Middle of the Book

for E.G.

From the starry gutter of the book
she looked up, out the window
which at that moment was levitating
the grass,

and the story rested
or continued—

lost in juniper, or childhood,
or childlessness,
the snap of the roof—

night falling in its black lanugo.
If you stared at night
your child would be night,
and if you meditated on a painting
of a monkey your child
would resemble a monkey
or if you craved cherries the child
would carry the birthmark

and so on and so on

and then
this is the story: the woman
in the first chapter has dreamed
she had a son and, in the part
that is not a dream, the boy is
a wolf. And in the next chapter,

the main character is a meadow,
where the part of the boy that is
wolf was found.

It is a story without progress,
like the imagination

or the body.

three

Annunciation

They say it happened
during unauthorized experiments by the operators.

They say conception
was a draught of wind, the will
of an angel blew the dome off
the reactor.
                The countryside was drunk at the time.
Bulls staring at the usual walls while,

for a moment, the whole of April had gone
female around them. . . .
When at last

a witness showed up, the windows were
knocked out, the old maternity hospital

was littered with glass and metal instruments
too radiant to touch—
wormwood bushes blackening over the steps—

It's the way new lovers
say it happened: like a blinding, like a blast.
And yet all through it someone
was able to write poetry. And later,
someone came to record,

to interview the old woman and photograph
her goat-mule,
the freak offspring of the abandoned farms—

She said, in rough translation,

Who you turn to
when your town burns up,
                                   well, that tells you everything.

The Life and Times of Skin Girl

I

She decided to follow the gods home
in their gownlike T-shirts and shaved skulls.

Twilight was still a feather.

The blood pumped hard in their radio,
it said, sex kings sex kings,

as objects turned to their blueness slowly
and, slowly, the world of the eye was leaving
and coming into the world of the hand. . . .

Soon she lost the toss of their shadows
in the calving darkness,

the last shrew cricket falling finally off
the night's steep magnitudes.
And suddenly, there,

at the corner, they went in. And were nightingales.
Where was the field of mercy?
Where were the ambrosial drops in
the cup of hours?

Midnight: One light so shimmery
they had to undress for it—

all nipple and seam and near human.

They had stopped
singing. Could be birds no more. Took off
their soft

sleeves, took out the silver
beads from their tongues . . .
and the beads like seeing beings sat.

2

As if she'd gone down into the dead,
there was no one to come and lead her back.

But all the light she'd need was at
their fingertips: One with his thumb
scratched the match head alive, threw

the flame to the floor where it blueballed out.
This, he said,
for the bitch who thought my world too dark
and frightening, too atomic and unkind. . . .

That's all she'd need to fall in love with death—
to believe he was merely misunderstood

while his minions lay on mattresses,
snakes on their backs.
Roses.
Lightning bolts.

What time was it?
Where was the well to bring up infant souls?
Truant waters . . .

Mostly they slept and reminisced and sailed
their brief matches in the lap of blackness.

It was a game of dedication: This, one said,
for the bitch who put words in my mouth.

3

She could smell weed and clove
and see one of them coming to the window
by the Day-Glo alien doll
hung around his neck. It was green
as ice. He,

the void over which its small face moved.
And the void was the night
she passed out in the railroad tracks among the cellophanes

the candy-ravers crushed and left,
and the Star Express came roaring. The night

that Lala Petite had stuck her head in
a woofer during the dope rave at the Nile.
That night the gods so loved the world
they let

anyone in for five bones and
then let the One Singing lift her up
to the light at the mouth of the place—candles

shrining a framed picture of the Dalai Lama.
And then the train.
A thousand lamas blazing.

4

Looking is the only great thing the gods do.
Otherwise, sheer boredom. Sheer world.
Same transparent ache of having
named everything. Everything being their child,
their dumb, deaf child.

It is this way: Everything
in the window is out the window.
Her face

leafed slowly through the black air
as his eye turned her—sight
and memory shuffling

the looked-upon. She moved back.
The remembered-after.
She turned.
The looked-after.

That feeling of streaming from looking.
That whole gold snakedom—

5

When she finally stopped running and was
seated in the stiff orchidean light of
the Pancake House, halos hunched over
two stacks and a side as she watched

the boy in the hair net turn back into steam
until nothing was left but the luminous
patch of the coffee cup and the whole
pleasing punk of the place . . .
the house music, breakbeat and trance—

She looked out
into the drosophilas' frenzy like some
weird fizz up the picture glass.

It was the nightmare of the seconds.

6

The spirits: How is it to live in the world?

The bodies: Who lives in the world?

White moment of the morning, that cool-sheeted air and not having slept.
And not having slept, she felt she had come from somewhere secret and distant
and not entrusted to just anyone.

The parking lot set with tourmalines.

And not entrusted to anyone.

There were times when the light felt like a look, just taking in her face,
dwelling on her hair.

This was as good as a god gets.

The god being
one who never turns around.

Souls

The body covered with faces, the
hipbone face, the nipple face, knee face,
and the upside-down black face of each eye. . . .

As if the human
were a glitter

or a train of portraits . . .

It's possible then the white gaze of my shoulder
belongs to an ancestor, or
one of my many demons

who mostly wants to stay in bed all the time
and quote Mandelstam,
"When I am old may my sadness gleam."

Or ask,
What were the chances

I'd live most of my life across
the street from a church, an old-fashioned
one, that still rings out on the hour

so that the soul can say to the body,
I am in the bells.

Lost Tribe

Blond as a basket, big-headed, the wolf-messiah
born in the village
is buried quickly—

Spit thrice in the hole and pat
the dirt,
the story to tell is it was just

her nerves. A little rest,
a little soup. Oh, not every time
a woman swoons

is it a case of fertility.
The ongoing wound
she is—
Though at night in the hills
such a chorus, shrill,
osmotic—the shirt-tearers,

the hair-twisters, the holy
sleep-skinners,
the yiy-yiy-yiy-yiy-ers
the dum-dai-diddle-
dum-dai-ers, the vuh-vuh-vuhs. . . .

This is how the spirit came to me,
swank and elegiac,
ready to kiss another
century or two.

Of course, from love
we come back to time—

who makes the last thing last.

Burn Boy's Celestial

On television Burn Boy had seen the moon
more than once. And sex at least twelve
thirteen if you count Japanimé.

His favorite commercial was local,
the fat bearded guy in bermuda shorts
wearing a cowboy hat and holster.

Burn Boy's mantra was *Next*.
The night he torched some asshole's
wood bird feeder and booked for *Twilight Zone*,

next rinsed himself in weed
and went lotus on the couch all night
he controlled the vertical he controlled the horizontal

he wished himself into the lamp
in a motel room in a rerun cop drama
clear sky out that night and a low moon—

neon vacancy
sixty million viewers like the stars
and he imagined the television gazing up at him

thinking how easily the motel would burn
the smolder of the stiff gray carpet
the crack of a commode unsealing

and all those Bibles—Through the valley of.
Begetting. And the Lord said—
And his smile was good

as he clicked from the cop to D4
playing "Get Loose," drummer shirtless,
cymbals a-tiddle. A fine world,

a fine world, he thought, comes right in,
busy sky he can turn green or orange
or back or forth from terminal illness

to flyfishing to weather to fucking-standing-up.
He wanted to die with the TV on.
He wanted the rapture to lick him up

like a warehouse blaze just starting
to eat the street.

Torture Boy's Cradle

Since Torture Boy had buried the rabbit
there was no love left. It was a secret
like his mother's voice behind the bedroom door
or the way his Dad and his nightly brandy
stared at nothing. Cruelty could be
believed, that was its comfort. He'd grown then,
grown then right out of the droop of body,
the indifference it had so finally. The listlessness.

Sometimes at the dinner table
there'd come a knock, a knock. Father
would say, *That's the boys under the floor,
they want your peas.* And he'd be twinkling.

From talking he'd come back and see
his glass was empty. *They were thirsty,*
his father said.

Sometimes when he reached for bread
his father'd pin his hand with a fork
and he'd say *Please—*

Later there'd be music from the living room
and he'd slip out and look for something
to poke. Something to skin out
of its pretty camouflage and sparkle.
It was always Rachmaninoff, it was always
the Kingston Trio, it was always "Red Roses
for a Blue Lady," nothing but storm and croon
and love. It pissed him silly. The violins
with their silvery guts, the harmonies, the tunes.
It was just as bad as blood he couldn't stop.

Mourning is not perfect. And Torture Boy
mourned. His knife was nothing.
Bring back the Judas' Cradle, The Pear,
the Heretic's Fork, instruments of true
understanding of the point
at which a living thing gives up itself
to pain in a sexual exhaustion strung out
past any fabulous attenuations of desire,
like a cloth undone with the polishing.

The Set Glistening

It was then I thought I heard someone
say there were birds in the library.
I knew it was autumn.

I knew in such a season
books were flying open, open

for days and then suddenly shut
like rooms into which half

a heated argument has gone.
I was wrong.

I had misheard the voices completely.
The only real understanding was in
the cocked head of the crow
pacing the green car's rooftop

as I walked a little farther and
everything became a little later,

time and distance, the ribs of the encyclopedias,
the pushiness of the whispers,
hush, you're not supposed to

be fully alive yet: This is the place of books,
the shooting up, the twittering, the preening,
the middle-of-the-night and fabulous

concatenating calls, song slipknotting
the egregious minutes, the cooling dark—
It was then

I had nothing left to bless but my own mistake,
not a logical thing

like the soul, smart enough not to inhabit
the body, but living in the nearby

rock or owl and eating at its separate table.
And the time, as it is set glistening on that table,
is different from the time we wait for
over here.

There was a time when there were scarlet
tanagers rustling behind the shelves,
and the Russian poets

left at their table, one still asking,
Who shall I tell my sorrow,
my horror greener than ice?

Sometimes I have nothing left to praise
but someone's sorrow.

Which is like my sorrow, which is like
the perfect and severe whistle of the bird
smart enough

to stay out of our heads—stay up all night
reciting the law codes

which it does from pure memory,
greener than ice. In the deep

accident of my ear. Mine alone,
the joy of surviving twice the same
mistake—

one more time and no one will remember
that wasn't the way it went,
the original song, it went like

the larks were stars and the mountains
were Bibles and whatever was said
was said between them.

Warning

This put-out eye
mother always warned against
when you ran with your fork

and its speared beet slice.
This
light from the blood,

Skin Girl,
is Hope. Like that:

a burst-vein-colored window
you can eat like an icicle—

Brother Tongue,
you'll have an accident
like speech.

Nights with the Star-Ladle over the House

Who now
leaves the door open a crack,
the hall light, the mother light,

the Light-All-Night
planting its straw of sleep?

Don't be sad when the drifting begins,
no one to talk
water to the glass,
rim to the window.

It's an ordinary life—
And to this angel

the whole body is throat.

And the two worlds—
are they still there, world

of the guarded, world of the guard—

First you're one,
then you're the other.
But you're the other the longest . . .

That's what the light meant.

four

Memory on the Shoulders of the Gaze

As you enter the museum there is a gate
covered with photographs
clearly from another time—when
the camera could only capture the conversation
between light and the several darks.
The village, of course, was destroyed.
The people were taken somewhere.
The animals stayed behind—and lived
in the local portrait studio which was
by mere accident
the only building left standing—
faces all over the floor,
the floor looking, the animals
walking—the sun going down
like a gray clay
and the lives of mothers and their children
and the lives of children and their wolf-pets
and the curious fur hats
behold the way you go—
the way you are returning, alien
because you live,
because you always knew memories
were sons-of-bitches, secret dogs
who watched them torture and burn.

Warning (2)

In a fire near the river,
a wolf burned the hair off his face
back to the pink creature—

They were drinking and they threw on
gasoline. They were howling
and unnerving the spirits—if
there were spirits—

They were only boys, new
at atrocities.

Don't ever come close.
Don't ever be fascinated
or they'll push you in.

You'll come home
unrecognizable, like the dead—
everyone at the dinner table

passing the salt past you. Glitter.
Whiteness. *Oh,*

how we loved you, starry eye.

The Torture and Burn Boys Entered the Video Arcade

Move over, geek—
they said, This is our game.

The lights blinking like candies, red
cinnamon buds and silver drawer pulls
and bright green fizz-beans

timed to the electric yips and cha-bongs
of some genius with an earring in his eyebrow
kicking cyberass

and saving Skull Lord.
The boys were hot—
it was a holiday,
the Feast of Yarrows—
hands on the joysticks

exploding blue strobe-finches from
the fallout of the pixels and the trees,

Burn Boy flipping back his satin bangs,
all twitch now, playing
Baked Revenge, Kingdom of O's, Heartstopathon.
Then Buzzarding the Meadow—

Again, and again twice.
Beat that—

and the other said,
Watch this, fucker.

And he said, Yeah, I'm shakin'.

So he said, Bite my big one. And
he said, Fuck you. Then
the other said, Fuck you. So he
said, Fuck you,

and the brotherhood was complete
and not long

after their starry numbers came up:
24 kills apiece, the all-time
third-highest

after 25 scored by player Ezra LB.,
and the record,
29, held by the player who went by the name
Wolf Boy,
King of Thebes. . . .

Twentieth-Century Children (5): Blood-Kissing

The boy in the girl's ear says, Kiss me until
  you draw blood.

And she's the hot thorn on his lip.

Stars wince and swell and wet,
  endless little cut-me's . . .

Through the night the great sponge of traffic,
  the oozy distance, the radios, the malls,
  the cat survivalists

living out of a hole in the library.
Someone

has to say it: Nail me
  to you.

The girl has always loved like suicide.

And the kiss wants to
  know, Am I deep enough—

Am I lord and cock-ring
  and ruby hammer,

spike and sundering thing?

The black place in the skull saying,
  Infect me. Be not only *Other*
  but *It*.

The way desire is—
  live rat sewed up inside us.

Forest-Body (2)

As if light is
the conversation that stops
when I appear,
that's what it's like to wake—

Good window, remember
this side

is the adoring one, the other
forgetful, fitful, birds

rising, letting slip their
iridescent robes. It would be all wrong
if the grass or the yellow

gateflower spoke now. Ravisher,
remember
this is skin city,
sheer curtain swaying, and the dead
and the living can both say,
Their silence is heaped on our silence . . .

Meaning each other.
Meaning and swaying—

Memory
populates us
with its redundant beautiful tree.

Nights in the Constellation of the Tree Stepping from Its Robe

for Norman

Like a star or a stick suddenly given
the way to say everything it held in so long,
the leaves fall
open from the tree, says the dream, like yellow kimonos. . . .

Thank God here
we're the only ones who speak,

not the wooden chest, the blue ginger-jar lamp,
not the shoe going under the bed,
not the tree stepping from its robe,
though it seems if anything had the right. . . .

I wake from where
there's no such thing as mute. Each thing has

its lament, its refrain,
its sustaining gibberish.
Oh kiss and kiss and kiss, says the boat
floating from that dock of rickety dark . . .

And only now
I feel ashamed, burning off
that word-life, as if only now
the quiet room can hear again.
Nothing says, welcome. Nothing says, lost,

adrift, daft, bedizened, daughter—
though I've come

from that country
where the simple sheet of paper whispered,
Bread. And bread

said, Mist.
And last—

Last night the *shochet's* axe poured its blessing over
the hen's stretched neck:

Between poetry and justice, choose justice,
between poetry and desire, choose desire,
between poetry and death,
choose death, because you have no choice.
Only when there is nothing else,
fight for poetry.

Hummingbird

In your little deafening,

the days
are getting longer, no matter
who speaks to you—

Only your green spark
cries out. And then it's night.

In sleep
part of the brain stays awake
always listening,
the God-spot.

Both of us out there
poking for dream food. You know

this world
the way I know the moment
a woman riding

alone in an elevator closes
her eyes and murmurs
a wish—

The grave petals open.
But not from knowing.

Life Story

When I read to the wolf boy,
he fell asleep right during the part
the kingdom's sky began to brood and
lightning jimmied the great amethyst doors
open through the dark—

He dreamed there was a village
of things ajar that sons peeped out from,
and he could see
the women in their kitchens
making wolf pie.

And if he woke,
they'd die; and if he slept until morning,
they'd forget,

the ovens would cool . . .
or something burning

would follow his life burning, and he'd
turn, and he'd never quite see
what it was—

fairy tale, fairy tale,
memory or recipe,

musk in the mouth,

I snap off his lamp into
his breath—ah,

small leaving thing,
the rain isn't falling—
it is cleaved.

Summer Heats like the Needle in Its Chosen Skin

And hummingbirds flung into the air,
fistful of violet amphetamines—

The clear water of the sky
as it dusks.

The ground, the road tar, the rock,
as if they know fever, know
the mouth that keeps coming

to the belly—
wolf-mouth

and the boy who shimmers out
on the balcony tonight blinking
strychnine and gold tracers,
passion vine

staring in the pool those blossoms
never come up from,
little humanities. . . .

Let's go out in the desert and shoot things,
June Boy says.

Let's tie up a dog on the freeway.

Watch
the lights trying to say *turn away,*
burn away

to the stink of ethanol and piss.
As if mystery

was asking for it.

Sudden Masters

for Miguel Murphy

Blood,
I dreamed I held your dark head against my breast.
I comforted you.

The next day a man said
—I dreamed they hacked off my father's arm
and his eyes were blinded
with blood,
and then there was someone

holding out his own grimy heart
like a car part and
my little sister saying he was
a fool for taking it out—

Right now, I'm thinking when the desert nights
cool, at last, and very slowly
in October, I'm thinking, and I'm interrupted by that white
shaved three-quarter moon

clearing the acacias that screen
my house from the neighbor's junked yard,
a sink tossed on the gravel
and a mysterious bin of colored golf balls,

I'm thinking that love is no good
without pity.

Without pity, it's horror:

the cut sex shining alone in our palms,
the spilling, the irreparable harms
and the helpless murders in our bed.
Then we sleep:

And Lobe, Tongue, Nipple, Bright Sheath,
the loved rise up again, against us,
and then they are knifed and then they are
blinded, and then they are in us,

trees, nicked moon, sudden masters of disguise
and resurrection:

Someone holding out his grimy heart—

the dream a flood
up to the level of our oldest bodies, those
sexual otherlings
shedding the violence of the private. . . .
Oh, Arms,

this death
was so wide, my father was not there,
just as he is not in this life,

that's how vast a world is. The spirit
doesn't leave the body, it has nowhere
else to go. It eats

a hole in the body. It burrows in,
it crawls, and teems, it mates for life—

all one has to do to the brain is
touch it, touch it,

and memory occurs. Speech is lost.
A man will believe he is a fork.

In the end, Heart,
my mother simply couldn't turn
my father over in bed anymore and his
own skin ate him. His own

blood poisoned him. His spirit
oozed. . . . Marvelous Iris—

the sodomites
with their hot chains fall upon you and you
never wake up.

Relic

for Beth

Wrapped in muslin, a ruby in each nostril
after the silver stick had stirred away
the brain and it oozed out and someone said
God bless—

the wolf looked
glued to death, its gleam
defunct and nasty, the belly fur
darkening like hemp.

The ears had been pulled off
long ago, by the boys who go tomb-hopping
Saturday nights, one in a T-shirt

that says *Torture*, the other in a jacket
that says *Burn*.

So much for religion. So much
for the love of calling hill to hill.

The tail wound with Tyrian purple and the eight
blackened nipples pierced with hammered tin—
What kind

of kingdom was this, where they ornament
their beasts like brides—before
or after they scoured out the heart?

The Courtship at the End of the Book

The trick: knowing
someday I'll only want to be here,
the acacias greening over in October
for the second spring—
what we call autumn in the desert.
Back yard

and the sound of the highway running
east and west at once,
late afternoon.

Late, Late Afternoon,
be the man in my life—

All arm, all breath, green lace
up to the sky. Mere tree.
Mere hour . . .

Sun and a backache and a dragonfly, what
ever does now, and does to me,
and wants more, and does it,

your hum is all I want to hear.
But say it. Say,

I'm the memory. I'm the one
wearing your big white shirt,

bearing the life of a trickster,
the red gold

that light lights through the lobes,
tips, lids, drops, all
mysterious ovens of the look—

all letters beginning, "Last night, my love,
last night . . ."

and meaning, "all we wanted. . . ."

Skin Girl's Tattoo

Wanting it dark, it deep, it blue
as the bitten place,

its bruisy effect, she chose
the diva of blossoms, dragonfire
of the Rose above her left breast

inking open in an endless
riff of itself and murmuring,
I'm your velvet—
                    the boy with
the metal lips bent over her,
gauzing up the little blood
with a chill of alcohol, and the skin
all quicks—
                    I could do a chapel like this.
                              And the Rose:
Are you leaving? Am I done?
Am I Yours Always?
                    Skin's girl rising,
bones clear as a current in a slipstream—
I eat when I want.
I wound where I want.
And I
        believe the only beauty
is the leap from the building
burning in our sleep to the real
enfolding darkness.

Washed in the River

Of course the woman with the mouse-child was famous,
as grace is famous,
a rarity

at the end of suffering. She kept him in
a nest in the dry bathtub
and washed in the river.

And though only children were meant
to believe this, I still believe this.
The fate of the body
is to confound

itself with everything. That's why
in another tale, the fair sister
opened her mouth and spoke
rubies,
and the plain sister, vipers and toads.
Meanwhile, the mother

of the gray thing
bathed him in a teacup.
Plucked him out and let him
run along the shore

to the window. Where both of them
were struck in longing—
he behind the great glass,
she behind the gray boy.

The second you see yourself in the suffering
the story's over.

Notes

"Easy": The lines "Why the grass . . ." are from John Donne's "Of the Progresse of the Soule."

"Last Erotica": "Cups of the eyelids, hinges . . . " is from Gerard Manley Hopkins.

"The Set Glistening": "Who shall I tell . . ." is from Marina Tsvetayeva.